BETTE WESTERA is the author of the Mildred L. Batchelder Honor Book *Later, When I'm Big* (Eerdmans) and over fifty other books for children. She has also translated books by Dr. Seuss, Astrid Lindgren, and Julia Donaldson into Dutch. Bette lives in the Netherlands, where her books have received two Golden Pencil awards and six Silver Pencil honors. Visit her website at bettewestera.nl.

MIES VAN HOUT is a Dutch illustrator and author whose work has been published in over twenty countries. Her books in English include *Happy, From One to Ten, This Is My Daddy!,* and *What Cats Think* (all Pajama Press). Mies lives in the Drenthe province of the Netherlands. Visit her website at miesvanhout.nl or follow her on Instagram @miesvanhout.

DAVID COLMER is an Australian writer and translator of Dutch and Flemish literature. He has translated over eighty books throughout his career, including *Little Fox* (Levine Querido), *I'll Root for You,* and *A Pond Full of Ink* (both Eerdmans). His translations have won many awards, including the PEN Translation Prize and the Independent Foreign Fiction Prize. David lives in Amsterdam.

Text © 2021 Bette Westera
Illustrations © 2021 Mies van Hout

Originally published by Gottmer, Haarlem, the Netherlands
under the title *Brave hond! Stoute kat! Versjes over de aard van het beestje*

Translation rights arranged by élami agency
English-language translation © 2024 David Colmer

First published in the United States in 2024 by Eerdmans Books for Young Readers,
an imprint of Wm. B. Eerdmans Publishing Co., Grand Rapids, Michigan
www.eerdmans.com/youngreaders

MIX
Paper | Supporting responsible forestry
FSC® C104723
www.fsc.org

Nederlands letterenfonds
dutch foundation for literature

Illustrations created with acrylic ink, oil pastels, and collage

The publisher gratefully acknowledges
the support of the Dutch Foundation for Literature.

FAST CHEETAH

SLOW TORTOISE

POEMS OF ANIMAL OPPOSITES

Bette Westera & Mies van Hout

translated by DAVID COLMER

EERDMANS BOOKS FOR YOUNG READERS

GRAND RAPIDS, MICHIGAN

Slow

No, no . . .
I'm . . .
not slow.

I just . . .
like . . .
to take . . .
my time.

— THE TORTOISE

Fast

Whish-whoosh!
See that?
Nope.
Too fast.

If you wanna see me,
you gotta be quick.

Whish-whoosh!
See me now?
No? Missed me again?

Too bad. Too late.
I'm outta here.

— THE CHEETAH

Cautious

What's that noise?
Is it a wolf?
A fox?
An eagle?
Watch out.
Stay in your hole.
It could be a bear.
Or . . .

Oh . . .
It's only Squirrel!

— **THE GROUNDHOG**

Reckless

No tree too tall,
no trunk too smooth.
I leap from branch to branch
and scurry through the bushes
in search of nuts.

Foxes don't scare me.
I just run rings around them.
I'm busy playing all day long
and don't see when it's getting dark.

Till Mama calls,
"Bright-eyes, where are you?"

Then I jump, spin around,
and start to run.
"Coming!"

— **THE SQUIRREL**

Tidy

I'm a neat little piggy
who keeps a clean pen.
It's always spick-and-span.

I never roll in my own muck
or anybody else's.
I only patter through the mud.

And then I scrub and scrub
until I'm clean.
And put a fresh curl in my tail.

— THE PIG

Messy

My hog house a pigsty?
What did you expect?
A cowshed maybe,
or a horse's stable?
Don't make me laugh!

Wash and comb my hair more often?
What for? Once a year is plenty.
These tangles suit me fine.

Zap my warts with Freeze Off?
What a terrible idea!
I love me just the way I am,
warts and all.

— THE WARTHOG

Obedient

It's so hot here on the hill!
We're baking in these woollies.
We want to go to a shady meadow
to eat some nice green clover.

Run away? Not us.
We'll just wait
until the shearer comes
to free us from our winter coats.

— THE SHEEP

Rebellious

That wooden fence?
I can jump over it. Look!

That nasty barbed wire?
I can squeeze through. See?

That weird pen?
Am I supposed to go inside?
I'd rather climb on top of it!

That feed? Is that for me?
Too smelly! I'll have carrots—
fresh from the garden!

— THE GOAT

Mean

Hey, you. Scram!
This is my ocean,
all of it.
Go and find your own sea
to swim in,
shark bait!

— THE LANTERN FISH

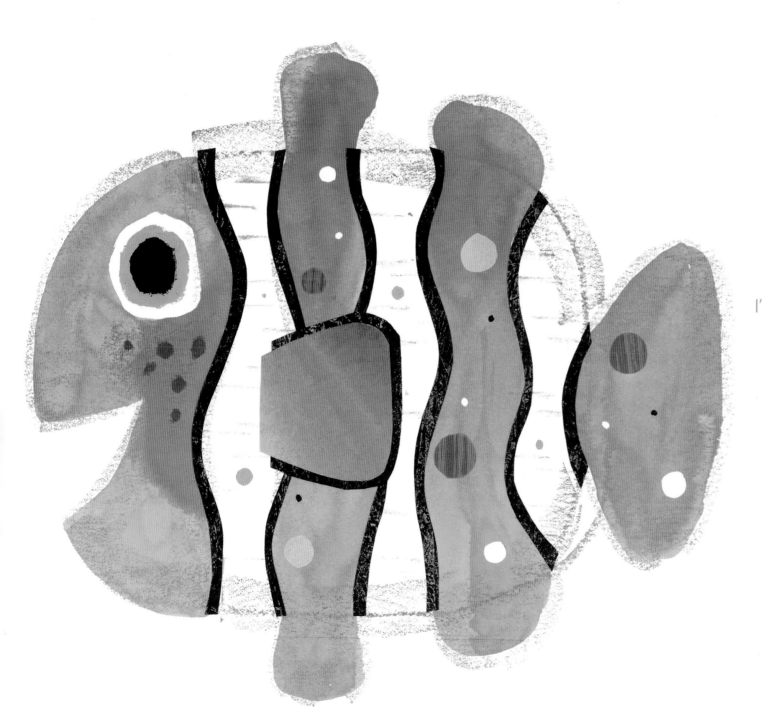

Friendly

Hello, little fish,
shall we play together?
We can look for seashells
and yummy water worms.
I'll take the tail and you can have
the head.
Or the other way round.
I don't mind.

It's my birthday soon.
If you like,
you can come to my party.

— THE CLOWNFISH

Patient

My web is ready—
now I just need
to bide my time
until a big fat fly
comes calling.

It might take a week,
or maybe two.
It doesn't matter.
I'm an expert
at lying in wait.

— **THE SPIDER**

Restless

Where shall I sit now?
On the windowsill?
The ceiling?
Or on that painting?
No, somewhere else . . .

That armchair looks comfy.
Or is the couch better?
The window?
The bookcase?
Maybe a table leg?
But there's four of them.
Which one?

I can't decide.
Know what?
I'll just fly around
a little more.

— THE BLOW FLY

Dazzling

Look at me!
Aren't I gorgeous
in my colored clothes?
Much better-looking
than the moth
and the bee
and the stick insect.
Don't you agree?

Look at me.
Admire me.
Pretty as a picture
on the wing!

— **THE BUTTERFLY**

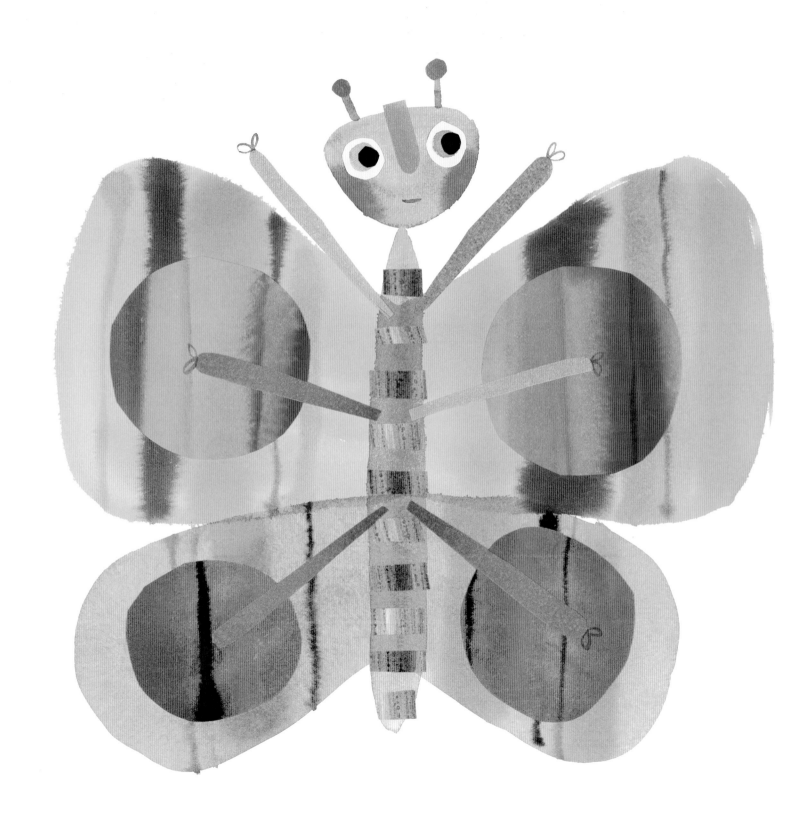

Plain

Shall we play hide-and-seek?
You can be *it*
because I'm sure
I'm a lot better at hiding
than you are.

One, two, three . . .
I'm hidden already! Can you find me?
Do you need a clue?
I'm as brown as the branch
I'm sitting on.
Hard, isn't it?

— **THE MOTH**

Naughty

I bite the potted plants
and use the chairs to sharpen my claws.

I stroll across the windowsill
and smash a vase
when I try to catch a butterfly.

I hunt mice and birds
and leave them on the doormat
as a present.

First I lick the butter in the dish,
then I knock the cat food
off the shelf.

And when my tummy's nice and full
I curl up on your lap and purr.
I am so sweet!

— THE CAT

Good

My master says, *Sit!*
and I sit down.

My master says, *Walk!*
and I pick up my leash
and run to the back door.

My master says, *Dig!*
and I start to dig,
until I've found a bone
to chew on.

My master says, *Drop it!*
and I drop the bone.
Good boy! my master says,
and gives me a treat.

— **THE DOG**

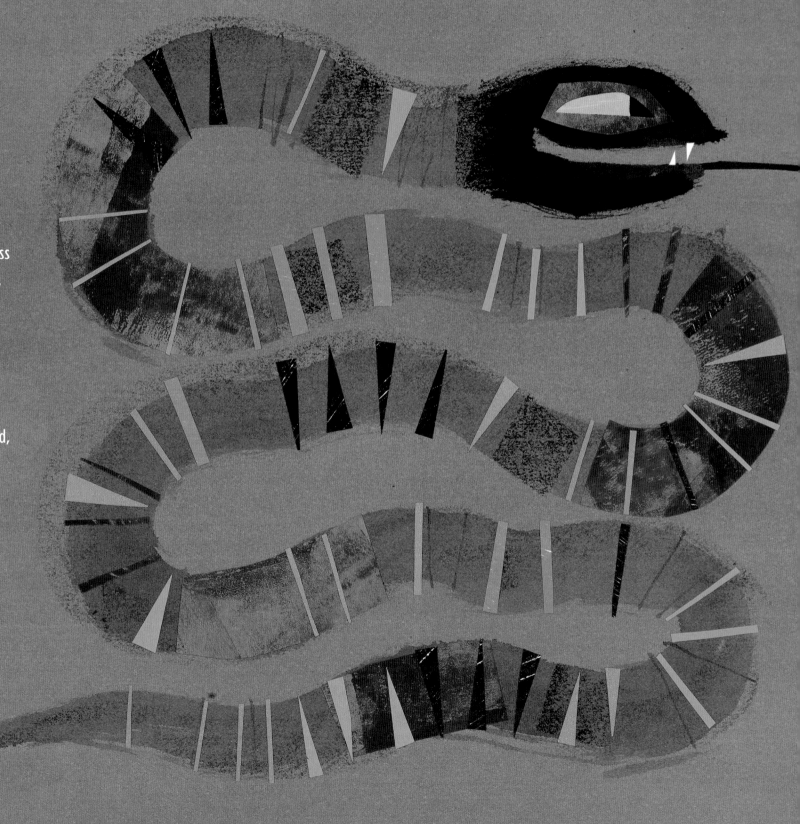

Dangerous

I slither through the grass
and sunbathe on a rock.
I'm not bad at heart,
but watch out!

If you tease me,
I'll start to hiss.
And if you make me mad,
I'll show you my fangs
and let you feel them!

— THE SNAKE

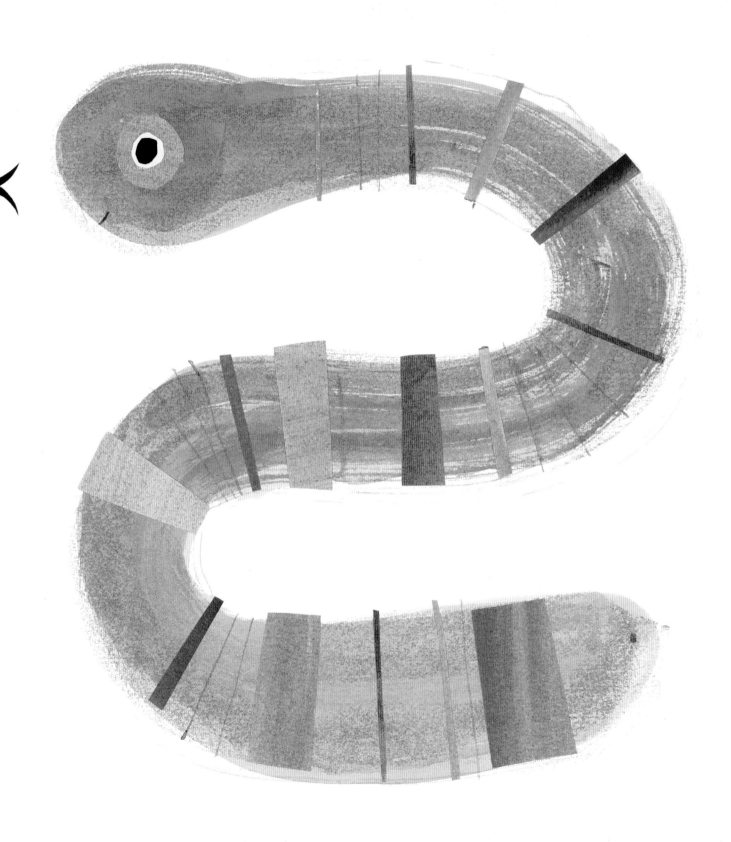

Harmless

No need to be afraid of me.
I wouldn't hurt a fly.

I don't eat bugs
or caterpillars.
Just autumn leaves.

All I do is dig
long tunnels
through the soil.

— THE EARTHWORM

Strong

I am the king
of the forest.
Don't think I'll
step aside for you.

You want to get past?
Go ahead.
I'll just
stand here.

— **THE MOOSE**

Delicate

I'm not imposing
like Uncle Elk.
Or stately
like Aunt Caribou.
I'm not as strong
as Uncle Moose.

I'm the smallest and shyest
of the whole family.
But I'm the fastest, too!

— THE DEER

Bossy

This is my forest,
and these are my trees.
If you want to swing on a branch,
ask me first.

I'll play tag with you,
but you have to be *it*.
And your little sister can't join in.
This forest is not for babies.

What's that you say?
You're going to get your mother?
Go on, get her.
And I'll get mine!

— THE GORILLA

Meek

Hi . . .
Could I maybe,
when you're finished playing,
have a turn on that ladder?

Could I,
when you've had enough to drink,
just get to that fountain for a sec?

And could I maybe also
have a tiny little piece
of that banana?

"What?
Did you say something?
Speak up a bit, will you?"

— THE LESULA

Playful

We're real ocean acrobats.
We jump out of the waves
in graceful loops.

Our water ballet is all splash and splatter.
Up and down
and up and down
and up and down . . .

And all the time we chirp and chatter.

— THE DOLPHIN

Dignified

I'm much heavier than a car
and bigger than a boat.
I don't swim fast,
but I'm great at diving.
And that's a good thing too
because my favorite meal
is squid.

And guess where I
find them?
Way, way below,
on the seabed!

— **THE SPERM WHALE**

Fancy

A quick look in the mirror:
very chic, this red collar
over those dark blue feathers.
And how do you like my tail?
The peacock pales by comparison!
Sky blue and cloud white,
a lovely combination.
Hey, that feather's crooked.
I'll just straighten it out.
There, that's better.

— **THE TURKEY**

Everyday

I don't like frills
and frippery.
I don't like fancy
showing off.

I don't need a purple crest
or a bright orange tail.
When it comes to feathers,
just give me grayish brown
or brownish gray.

— THE CHICKEN

Relaxed

I like
to take
things
easy

and I love
just
hanging
on a branch.

But I'm not lazy.
Not at all.
The nine fingers
I hang from
are always hard at work!

— THE SLOTH

Busy

We're very hard workers.
We never take a break.
The idea of not having
anything to do
doesn't bear thinking about!

Thank goodness,
we don't have time
to think about it.
We're way too busy
for things like that!

— THE ANT

Noisy

I chirp the same song every day.
Hang on—I'll teach it to you.
It's very easy.
Just rub your wings together.
Chirr, chirr, chirr!
What's that? No wings?
Use your hands then.
Chirr, chirr, chirr!
That's right, but louder.
Chirr, chirr, chirr!
Excellent. You've got it!

— THE CRICKET

Quiet

We don't scratch,
we don't crunch,
we don't hum,
we don't buzz.

We sit under our rock,
and if we come out,
we sneak.

— THE PILL BUG

Contented

We like to stretch our wings
and sometimes we do go out.
But an hour of flying around
is plenty long enough.

We don't need to go to sunny climes.
Our cozy nests are good enough for us.

— **THE HOUSE SPARROW**

Adventurous

Come on, kids,
time to fly south!

The winter days are mild there,
the mosquitoes big and juicy,
and the flies all taste as sweet as
honey.

It never snows.
It doesn't freeze.

Sunshine on our feathers
the whole day long.
Lovely!

— THE SWALLOW